MORE HELP!
My Baby Came Without Instructions!

How to SURVIVE (and Enjoy!) Your Baby's FIRST YEAR

by
Blythe Lipman

More Help! My Baby Came Without Instructions!
by Blythe Lipman
Second Printing, 2008
Copyright © 2008

Library of Congress Control Number
2004097925

ISBN: 978-0-9762576-1-5

Edited by Paul M. Howey
Cover & interior design by Tina Lucurell
Illustrations by Shelley Dieterichs
Production by Buse Printing & Packaging

Help! My Baby Came Without Instructions!
First edition, October 2004

Published in the United States of America

DEDICATION

To my children...
Lindsay and Andrew

"Your book is wonderful. Being the mom of twin girls, I wish I'd had it when they were infants. It has lots of little suggestions that can make your transition into parenthood easier."

Melissa Capppello, mother of Alan and Sofia
Scottsdale, AZ

"What a wonderful, helpful and specific book. How nice to have suggestions and reassurances from an expert. I'd recommend this book to all new parents!"

Irma Ross MS, CPC, NCC
Norwalk, CT

"I am a grandmother of three boys and have asked Blythe for advice many times about teething, rashes, fevers, and other things. I loved reading her book and to this day, she still answers many questions and gives me advice I'd feel silly calling the pediatrician's office about! I encourage everyone to read this book and know they'll get the best advice from a knowledgeable source."

Nancy Polizzi, grandmother of three
Scottsdale, AZ

"Help…My Baby Came Without Instructions! *is a great book for new and second-time parents. Its advice is very thorough, giving multiple suggestions on a myriad of infant topics. As the author points out, there are many different ways to raise your child and usually, if your child is happy, you are doing it right."*

Craig Primack M.D.
Scottsdale, AZ

Blythe Lipman's book is a "must read" for all new parents! This easy-to-read guide is a great gift idea for a baby shower. Its helpful tips and practical ideas will calm and reassure even the most nervous new mom and dad. Sure wish it had been around when I had MY first baby!"

Sharon Edricks, M.S. — Educator and mother of two
Farmington, CT

"I have been delivering babies for over twenty years, and I can't tell you how many baby-care books have passed across my desk. I can't remember a single one that compares to Help! My Baby Came Without Instructions! *This book has incredibly valuable tips for new mothers, things I never would have thought of. I am going to recommend it to all my patients who are about to give birth and I highly and wholeheartedly recommend it to you."*

David M. Edinburgh, M.D.
Sharon, MA

TABLE OF CONTENTS

FOREWORD

As a practicing pediatrician with thirty year's experience, I was pleased to review Blythe Lipman's new book "More Help… My Baby Came Without Instructions!" It fills a necessary niche in parenting literature.

Before our society became so mobile, new parents had their extended family nearby. Especially the grandmothers who could transfer some of their child-rearing expertise onto their children. If a baby had a rash, grandmother was there to diagnose it, usually correctly. Whether it was teething, feeding, sleeping or developmental concerns, grandma came to the rescue!

Many of the young couples I now deal with in my suburban practice live far away from their extended families. Therefore, the pediatrician's office takes many of the phone calls that grandmother used to be able to help with. We see many infants with routine concerns because there is no other source of help available.

This book provides new parents a first-line reference. It is well-written, documented, full of practical, sound advice. I would recommend all parents in my practice have it at home, and call me only if their "Help" book couldn't answer their concerns. It is full of daily advice such as bathing and burping techniques, as well as addressing the frustration that can come when the baby won't eat or sleep.

I whole-heartedly recommend this book to all parents and child caregivers.

Alan B. Singer M.D.

ACKNOWLEDGEMENTS

I am grateful to so many people for helping me write this book that I can't catch my breath. Where do I begin?

Thank you, Gary, my partner in life. I could not have pulled this off were it not for your gentle nudging, your words of wisdom, for the hours you spent making my website, for your sense of humor when I was discouraged, for your gourmet dinners when I was too tired to cook or eat, and most of all, for your never-ending support and faith in me that I could actually write this book.

I am eternally grateful to my children, Lindsay and Andrew. You put up with other people's babies in our house for years. You never complained and you even helped me with them, not ever knowing—besides having fun—that you were the "Research and Development Department" for this book.

I lovingly thank my girlfriends, Nancy, Kathy, and Jo. You always let me talk and talk and talk about my book, my babies, my babies' parents, my tips, and everything else about my book. You never squawked when we went to lunch and I brought along a baby I was watching. You were never too busy to answer a question, share your honesty, or just offer your support. You unselfishly let it be about me. Now *that's* true friendship.

I am still in shock that I once again have my college friends back in my life after twenty-one years. Jan, Sharon, Irma, and Lisa, my book wouldn't have been complete without you. Your long distance editing, phone calls, e-mails, and suggestions, not to mention your great sense of humor all added more than you will know. Thank goodness we aged so well, and still like each other!

And then there were all the parents who gave me the honor of being part of the first years of their babies' lives. Thank you to them also for responding to my questionnaires and being part of my focus groups, sharing their pictures, trying my tips, and giving me daily reports. To Randy and Hart for letting me get my baby fix by caring for Jordan and Sydney and letting me try my latest tips on them. I love you all!

Thank you Sara and Anisah for practicing all my tips in our Infant Rooms. And to Beth and Lenny, for letting Pammy be the first baby in my life. For letting me squirt her in the eye with the bottle and lighting that spark at eleven years old. My love for babies started with that first bottle!

I have no false pride to think that I completed this book without the help of my medical friends, Dr. Primack, Dr. Kail, Dr. Fischler, Dr. Ziltzer, Dr. Edinburgh and Dr. Grunfeld. They checked and rechecked my tips and offered their knowledge after their many years of experience. Thank you, Dr. Singer, for your many years of baby instructions with my children. Without them and you, this book might never have been born.

And to Paul M. Howey, my wonderful editor, who made my words flow like music.

Shelley Dieterichs, my illustrator, whose pictures made my heart smile.

And to Ray Buse and Company, who made the delivery of this

book so easy, there wasn't one labor pain!

I am forever thankful to you all. Just by knowing you, I feel as though I've won the lottery.

Blythe

INTRODUCTION

So you did it. You are now the proud owner of a cute, cuddly baby. You've waited your whole life for this day, finally, you are officially a mommy. But now everyone has gone home. Grandma, grandpa, brothers, sisters, family, and friends have all left. While they were with you, they "oohed" and "aahed" and held and fed the baby. While they were with you, they let you take a nap, go out to dinner, take a shower, and have quiet time when you needed it. But now? Now *you are all alone* with this tiny, helpless, adorable *crying* baby. You are alone and in charge and suddenly you realize, "My baby came without instructions. Help!"

Relax. This book is designed to provide tips to make life easier for you, your husband *and* your baby. The first thing you need to know; there is no right or wrong way with most things when it comes to taking care of a baby. Some things work for one baby, and some different things work for others. One mother's way may be different from another (or even different from daddy's way of doing things). But as long as the baby is happy, you are doing it right. Babies are just little human beings who want to eat, sleep, play, be warm, dry, and comfortable. The problem is they cannot care for themselves. Nevertheless, they aren't as fragile as they may appear to be. What's more, they don't have a clue that you are new at this.

I have taken care of infants for more than twenty years and have successfully tried every tip in this book. Try one of the tips, try two, try them all, whatever makes you and your baby happy. Just know, as long as you relax, love, and marvel at this beautiful little bundle of joy, your heart and your baby's heart will smile.

I hope you enjoy my book and most of all enjoy every minute you spend with your baby, because (as you will soon discover) time sure flies and before you know it, these days and nights will be just a memory.

Blythe

Contact Blythe at: babyinstructions@cox.net
www.babyinstructions.com

"This book is a "must read" for every new mother! I read every baby book I could find when I had my first child and not one of them gave the practical, sensible and no-nonsense advice on taking care of baby that this one does. I wish I'd had this book at my fingertips during the first year with the baby. It would have saved many a sleepless night! I wholeheartedly recommend this book to every mother—new and not so new (and to every grandmother and future grandmother as well!) It has tips that most of us never would have thought of. The book is clear, concise, and an easy and handy reference that you will want to consult over and over. Buy one for yourself and one for each of your friends!"

Janis Edinburgh, J.D.
Sharon, MA

Turning Off Those Tears

TURNING OFF THOSE TEARS
What to Do When Your Baby Won't Stop Crying

Babies cry for lots of reasons. They cry when they're tired, hungry, too hot, too cold, over stimulated, not stimulated enough, wet, soiled, or sometimes just for no reason at all. What makes it difficult, especially if you're new at parenting, is that they can't tell you. If they are tired, they don't act sleepy; they act cranky. If they are wet, they don't point to their diaper; they act cranky. The following tips may help your cranky, crying baby feel better.

- Put a receiving blanket into the dryer for a few minutes to get it nice and warm. Swaddle the baby and lay her down in the crib on her side so her back is touching the crib or use

a wedge (see *Glossary*) or a rolled-up receiving blanket. Babies are accustomed to close quarters and feel secure when they are in small spaces.

(Note: While babies do come in two genders, my usage of "her" and "she" throughout this book is merely for simplicity. It is my intention that you have your own child in mind when you read my tips).

- Put the baby into a swing. Get a receiving blanket (again, you may want to warm it up in the dryer first) and pull it up between the baby's cheek and hand so she can touch it and feel the soft fuzziness next to her cheek. This is very comforting. You may want to put another rolled-up receiving blanket against her ear to hold it in place.

- Put the baby into the Exersaucer® (see *Glossary*) and show her all the fun toys mounted on the tray. If she is almost sitting up by herself, she is old enough to play in this type of toy. You may want to put a rolled up receiving blanket behind her back for more support, especially when she is first starting to play in this toy.

- Place the baby on her tummy lengthwise on your knees. Gently rock your legs while rubbing her back or patting her bottom.

- Put the baby into the bouncy seat (see *Glossary*). Some bouncy seats have toys attached. If yours does not have toys, put the bouncy seat in front of a mirror and let the baby look at herself. (Make sure you put her on the floor to look at herself and not on a counter, as the seat could fall off.)

- Pull a soft blanket or stuffed animal up to touch the baby's cheek or hands while in the crib, swing, or bouncy seat. It simulates being close to Mommy. You can even use one of your T-shirts; there's nothing more calming than a mommy's familiar scent! You can use a rolled-up receiving blanket to make sure the soft fuzzy blanket, stuffed animal, or T-shirt stays in place and does not cover the baby's face.

- Gently stroke the baby's forehead and cheeks with your fingertips as though they were feathers.

- Some babies like their heads covered with a blanket. Use a crocheted blanket with big holes and don't cover her nose or mouth. Just pull it up so the end drapes over her forehead and the back of her head is completely covered.

I have used this with older babies who roll over and like to sleep on their tummies.

- Make sure the baby isn't cold. Feel her nose and ears. If they are cold, add another layer of clothing or another light blanket.

- Make sure the baby isn't too hot. If you are hot, and the baby is dressed in long sleeves and is cranky, there is a good chance she is too warm, too.

- The baby might have gas. Burp her. If you tried burping her while you were sitting, stand up and walk. Sometimes a change in position will help bring up that gas bubble.

- If the baby had less to eat than usual, try a little more bottle. Even though she only ate an hour ago, sometimes a baby is not satisfied. Just as we sometimes need that piece of chocolate!

- Make sure those adorable clothes with bows and buttons and zippers aren't cutting into the baby's neck or arms. While those headbands look really cute, the elastic may be too tight on her head.

- Make sure the diaper is pulled out between her legs (where the elastic is). It could be pinching those little legs.

- Walk outside with the baby. Fresh air and new sights can be distracting enough so she forgets to cry.

- Put the baby in a warm bath, pour water gently over the back of her head, and sing a song.

- Hold the baby upright, facing you and supporting her head, if needed. Gently lift her up and down repeatedly. (This is great for your own upper body strength, too.) You can also sit on a fitness ball (see *Glossary*) and try this same maneuver.

- Put you baby in the bouncy seat and place it on top of the dryer and turn the dryer on. (Make sure you stand there.) The vibrations can be soothing, as well as distracting.

- Turn on the radio, fan, or vacuum cleaner. Once you find which noise is calming to your baby, make a tape recording of it.

- Put her in front of a mirror and show her the pretty baby.

- Sing to her.

- Wet a washcloth with cool (not ice cold) water and wipe the baby's neck and cheeks.

- Show the baby your dog, cat or fish.

- Put the baby into a Snugli® or Sling (see *Glossary*) and get on with your activities.

- Put the baby into her car seat and drive around. The motion is very soothing.

- Put the baby into her stroller and take a walk either inside or out. The sounds, smells, and scenery, along with the movement of the stroller, might make her feel better.

- Invest in a musical mobile for the crib. Put the baby into the crib, turn on the music, and watch her enjoy the motions and sounds.

- Make sure the baby doesn't have a little piece of string or hair wrapped around her little finger, cutting off the circulation. And check to make sure a zipper isn't pinching her neck.

- Give the baby a pacifier (binky) (see *Glossary*). If she has a hard time keeping it in her mouth, use a rolled-up receiving blanket. Put the blanket between her shoulder and ear, resting it next to her cheek and mouth so the pacifier won't fall out as easily.

- Standing, hold the baby on your left shoulder while swaying and patting her back. The sound and vibration of your heart is very soothing.

- Sit in a rocking chair and gently rock baby while patting her back and softly singing.

- Above all, don't get stressed. The baby can feel your tension. Sometimes a baby just cries even though nothing is wrong. Don't feel guilty. The baby isn't crying because you are not a good parent. Sometimes, babies just need to cry. She will stop, I promise you. When you're certain there's nothing wrong with your baby, just turn on some music, the television, or do something that makes you happy and relaxed. Before you know it, those tears will be dry!

Why Mothers Cry

"Why are you crying?" he asked his mother.

"Because I'm a mother," she told him.

"I don't understand."

His mother just hugged him and said, "You never will!" Later the little boy asked his father why his mommy seemed to be crying for no reason.

"All mothers cry for no reason," was all his father could say. The little boy grew up and became a man, still wondering why mothers cry. So he finally put in a call to God, and when God got on the phone, the man said, "God, why do mothers cry so easily?"

"You see, son," replied God, "when I made mothers, they had to be special. I made their shoulders strong enough to carry the weight of the world, yet gently enough to give comfort. I gave them an inner strength to endure childbirth and the rejection that many times comes from their children.

"I gave them a hardiness that allows them to keep going when everyone else gives up, and to take care of their families through sickness and fatigue without complaining. I gave them the sensitivity to love their children under all circumstances, even when their child has hurt them very badly. This same sensitivity helps them to make a child's boo-boo feel better and helps them share a teenager's anxieties and fears.

"And I gave them a tear to shed. It's theirs exclusively to use whenever it's needed. It's a tear for mankind."   -Author unknown

BABIES ARE SUCH A NICE WAY TO START PEOPLE.

This is the best book ever! The tips work like a charm and keep my baby content. The perfect baby shower gift...A must-have on every new parent's list!!

Beverly Freedman, Happy Mom
SkyLane, New Jersey

What a great book for Grandpas! Grandma was really impressed when I got the baby to stop crying! I would never watch my grandbabies without this wonderful book in hand!

Grandpa Gerson Pitel
Coconut Creek, Florida

Sweet Dreams

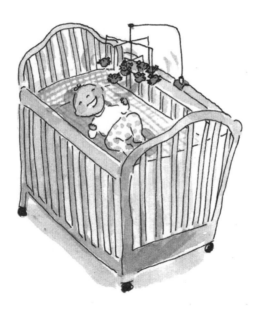

SWEET DREAMS
Sleep Time Made Easier

Ah, to hear that quiet breathing and those wonderful sleep noises on the baby monitor, a lullaby to any new parent's ears. But wait, do I hear crying? The baby has only been asleep for fifteen minutes. "But I'm so tired!" you wail.

Sometimes you can stand on your head, bring in a violinist or a whole floor show for that matter, and your baby will not go to sleep or stay asleep for very long. The following tips should bring the pleasant sounds of your baby snoring.

- Babies can sleep through anything. Get them used to the everyday noises in your home from day one. No tiptoeing or whispering. Turn that music on and dance to your heart's content.

- Put a receiving blanket into the dryer for a few minutes to warm it up and cover the baby with it. If she is a newborn, swaddle her in the warm blanket.

- When putting the baby into her crib, lay her on her side in the top left-hand or right-hand corner. Use a wedge or rolled-up receiving blanket to keep her on her side. It is very comforting for her to sleep with her back touching the side of the crib, wedge, and blanket. Remember, she is used to close quarters. To a baby, being in the middle of the crib is like being in the middle of the ocean!

- Tape some photos of mommy and daddy and even the family pets to the outside of the crib so the baby can see them. It is comforting for her to know the family is watching over her while she sleeps.

- Put your baby in a Snugli® or Sling (see *Glossary*) and go about your daily routine, vacuuming included.

- Make a recording of you and/or daddy singing lullabies and play them over and over for her.

- Rock her, but do it the same amount of time before each nap. Do not rock her until she falls asleep, just to relax her. (If you get into the habit of rocking her until she falls asleep, she may have a hard time going to sleep on her own.) Then give her a kiss, put her into the crib and turn on her music.

The Zoo

The funniest things happened when we were up all night with our newborn. He used to make noises, including snorts and squeals. My sister said it sounded like we were in the zoo and one night I could have sworn the baby said, "AFLAC"!

As told by Jon

- Put a ticking clock near the crib. The monotonous tick may soothe her to sleep.

- Put her into the stroller and wheel it around the house. The motion may make her sleepy. You don't have to move her if she falls asleep. Nap time is good most anywhere!

- Put her into the car seat or bouncy seat and cover her with a blanket or swaddle her, and then put the whole seat on top of the clothes dryer. Don't leave her! Stay with her and watch those heavy eyes. The vibrations are soothing.

- Swaddle the baby and lay her on top of the dryer on a blanket, or towel until she is lulled to sleep (again, you must stay with her). Then put her into the crib.

- Put her into the corner of the crib and gently stroke her cheeks with your fingertips.

- Put her into the crib and pat her bottom and softly say, "Shhh."

- Put her into the crib and gently rub her back.

- Put the baby into the swing and cover her with a warm blanket.

- Put the baby into the crib, place a pacifier in her mouth, and roll a receiving blanket and prop it next to the baby to keep the pacifier in her mouth.

- Give the baby a blanket or stuffed animal to touch. Put it close to her body and next to her cheek. Babies are very tactile little creatures, and she will find this soft touch to be very comforting.

- Put her into the bouncy seat with a vibrator (some bouncy seats come with a vibration option that gently massages the baby) and turn it on. Put the bouncy seat in the crib with baby sleeping in it. No need to disturb her.

The Birthday Present

Letting a baby sleep in bed with parents can have a downside! On my husband's birthday morning, he was greeted with his little princess having quite the poopy all over our bed. What a way to say Happy Birthday, Daddy!

As told by Alice

- Put her into the car seat and take a nice drive.. When she is asleep, bring her inside in the car seat. (No need to move her if she is sleeping like a baby.)

- Pick special music—lullabies, classical, whatever you like. Play the same music each time you put the baby into her crib to sleep. Be consistent, as this will teach her that when she hears this music, it's time to go to sleep.

- Buy a package of glow-in-the-dark binkys and scatter them in the crib within baby's reach.

- You can buy a stuffed bear that has recorded sounds from the womb including a heartbeat. The bear works on a timer making it easy for you. This bear is available at most toy stores and online.

- No matter how you choose to soothe your baby, make

It was time to bring baby Ashley home from the hospital. We safely strapped her in the car-seat, covered her with a blanket and took the short ride home. We were so excited about our newborn daughter. We brought in the car-seat with our adorable baby, sleeping peacefully. Suddenly it dawned on us, we were scared to move her. Baby Ashley spent her first night home sleeping in the car-seat!

As told by Todd and Kathy

sure you do it the same way each time. Consistency is the key to smiling babies (and parents).

"Blythe Lipman has been caring for my children for the last two years. Not only has she taught me everything I know, but, she has been there for me in all ways. She has helped me to relax, to understand what is going through my children's minds, and to enjoy the short time we all have with our children before they grow up and move out. I am the luckiest mommy in the world to know Blythe and I trust her wholeheartedly with all she does. Her book is an inspiration and I have tried every trick! They all work!"

Randy Robinovitz
Scottsdale, AZ

"Attention all new moms: Stop! Don't leave the obstetrics floor without this informative, interesting, and fun book! Everything a new mother needs to know is incorporated within these pages!"

Ronnie Grunfeld, mother of two
Scottsdale, AZ

Slip and Slide

SLIP AND SLIDE
Bathing Your Baby

Bathing your new baby can be very scary. Once the water hits her little body, it is a whole new experience. Slip, slide, and squirm are a few adjectives that come to mind. Just a few tips to make "Bath Time 101" a bit easier.

- Before you fill up any kind of tub, have the baby's towel (and all other supplies you might need) next to the tub.

- Fill the tub or sink with enough water to cover the baby's tummy. Before you put your baby in the water, test the water temperature with your elbow. It should be warm to the touch.

- Make sure all of the windows are closed and fans are turned off. The room should be free of drafts.

- Take the baby's diaper off last. Naked babies (as you will learn probably sooner than later) go to the bathroom anyplace. Don't be alarmed if she goes in the bath. This is very natural but sometimes frustrating when you have to start all over.

- Wash from the bottom of the toes up to the head. Some

babies don't like having their hair washed. Starting with tears is not fun.

- Buy a life-size rectangular sponge with indentations that look like the baby's body. This sponge will fit in the bathtub or a large sink. Fill the tub or sink with enough water to cover three-fourths of the sponge. Put the baby on her back so you have both hands free to soap, wash, and play.

- Use a small, plastic baby tub that will fit into your large tub. They make these tubs with fabric attached to the top and (like a hammock), extending from top to bottom on a slant. The baby's bottom is submerged in the water and the rest of her body is partially covered. You still need to support the baby with one hand, but you don't have to worry that her head will go under the water.

- Or put a large towel into the bottom of the sink and fill it with a few inches of water. While you support the baby's head and body with your hand, the towel will prevent her from sliding.

- When the baby can sit up, purchase a plastic bath chair. This seat attaches to the bottom of the tub with suction cups.

- When washing the baby's hair, hold a washcloth in front of her eyes while you rinse, to keep them dry and shampoo-free. Gently tilt the baby's head back and rinse using a plastic cup filled with warm water.

- There's even a product that looks like a circle of soft  plastic, almost looks like a sun visor that attaches around the back of the baby's head with velcro. This hat fits on top of the baby's head so you can pour water to rinse the shampoo away without it getting into her eyes.

- Picking baby shampoos or bath products is personal. Some contain aloe, lavender, roses, conditioner, and shampoo together, baby wash to relax the baby, etc. Try them all until you find one you and she like.

- Bubble bath sometimes irritates the baby's skin. As an

alternative, if you want to make bubbles, pour a small capful of shampoo under the running water.

- The bathtub is a great place to blow bubbles with a wand, for the baby.

- Take the baby out and put her onto a big towel, wrap her up, and give her a kiss.

- If you use powder, put it into your hand and rub it onto the baby. Never shake it directly on her body as it could get into her eyes, nose, mouth, and lungs.

- Don't forget to have fun washing, singing, and playing. There is nothing cuter than a squeaky, clean baby to make you smile.

NEVER, EVER LEAVE YOUR BABY UNATTENDED, NOT EVEN FOR ONE SECOND.
Accidents happen. There is nothing more important than your baby's safety.

Never Stand too Close with a New Suit On

Make sure you tell daddies that newborn babies pee when they are naked. On our first visit to the pediatrician, we had to undress our little baby girl, Jordan. Daddy had a brand new suit on and was very proud of his new daughter. As he was stood there, Jordan peed all over him! Even the nurse laughed!

As told by Randy

Feeding and Watering

FEEDING AND WATERING
The Keys to Successful Bottle and Breastfeeding

Deciding whether to bottle or breast-feed your baby is a truly personal choice. What's important is that you fill your baby's tummy with something nutritious when she is hungry. Don't listen to grandma, your friends, or the Lamaze instructor. Go with your gut!

LIQUIDS
1) Formula powder
a) Fill the bottles with water in the morning (most new babies drink between two to six ounces at each feeding). You can then leave the bottles out with the tops on, as water doesn't spoil. When it's feeding time, add the powdered formula. Follow the directions on the container, unless your doctor tells you otherwise. Put the cap on the bottle, shake it well until all the formula is dissolved, and feed. Most babies are not adverse to formula at room temperature. If she does not seem happy, try warming it for a few seconds in the microwave, in a bottle warmer, or in a cup with hot water. If you use the microwave, make sure to take the cap off first. When the bottle is heated, replace the cap, shake it (microwaves don't always heat evenly and the formula could get very hot on the bottom), and test it to make sure it's not too hot.

2) Canned Formula

a) Premixed formula is the easiest, but it's also more expensive than powdered formula. You just open the can and pour it into the bottle. Once you open the can, it is usually good for only 48 hours. It's hard to travel with big cans of formula because once it's opened, it must be refrigerated.

b) Canned formula that needs water added. This formula may be less costly than the premixed formula. Once you mix the bottles, they need to be refrigerated. This is hard to travel with (as once it's open, you must pour it into another container or it will spill). It is easiest to make the whole can. Once it's opened, there is only a 48-hour shelf life.

3) Breast Milk

a) If you breast-feed, you may decide to pump and store the milk, so you can have the convenience of sharing the feeding experience with daddy or a caretaker.

b) When you pump, store the amount the baby usually drinks (allowing one ounce more) into plastic bags labeled with the date and the amount in ounces. Put them in the freezer. When it's feeding time, take out the amount you think you will need defrosting it in a cup filled with hot water. (Don't heat the plastic bag in the microwave.) If the milk is already thawed and you want to heat it up, you may use the microwave. Pour the milk into a bottle and heat without the cap for a few seconds. Be especially careful if you do heat it in the microwave. As I mentioned earlier, not all microwaves heat evenly and so you need to shake the bottle and test the temperature before feeding the baby. If you know approximately how much the baby drinks in a day, it is sometimes easier to take the bags out each morning and store them in the refrigerator.

4) Water

Always have a bottle filled with water available. We all get thirsty. Most babies do not like ice cold water, so try room temperature. When it is hot, baby is a little cranky and it is not quite time for lunch, try some water. If you are giving a very young baby water for the first time, use a Stage One Nipple as water is much thinner than formula or breast milk and may take a little getting used to. This nipple has fewer holes so the liquid comes out in smaller quantities.

POSITIONS FOR FEEDING

Sit in a comfortable place, sofa, rocking chair, etc. Hold the baby in the position she likes.

- Maybe your baby will like to be in the crook of your arm with her head tilted up.

- Perhaps she'd prefer to be in the bouncy seat with you holding the bottle.

- Do not prop the bottle. The interaction at feeding time is very important and the baby could choke.

- Or you can prop the baby on a Boppy Pillow® (see *Glossary*) or a pillow with you holding the bottle.

- Never lay the baby flat to take the bottle, she must be in a vertical position to prevent ear infections and choking.

- Another way is to hold your baby in your lap, facing out, she can see what's going on in the rest of the room.

Of course, not all babies like to be held when they are taking their bottle (especially as they get older). It's important for both you and your baby to be content at feeding time. Just interact and enjoy the experience.

THE IMPORTANCE OF BREASTFEEDING

Breastfeeding is more than just another lifestyle choice—it's an important health choice for mothers and babies. Agencies that care about health support breastfeeding. The US Department of Health and Human Services, in cooperation with the Ad Council and La Leche League International, supports an ad campaign to promote breastfeeding that began in 2003.

PROTECTS BABIES FROM DISEASES

The frequency and severity of colds, ear infections, upper respiratory infections, and even chronic conditions such as asthma are all significantly reduced when children are breastfed. Breastfed babies suffer less from diarrhea, other gastrointestinal illnesses, pneumonia, sepsis, gastroenteritis, meningitis, and some forms of childhood cancer. Because of the reduction in frequency and severity of such illnesses, breastfed babies need fewer visits to the doctor.

Davis, M.K. Breastfeeding and chronic disease in childhood and adolescence. *Pediatr Clin N A* 2001; 48(1):125-41.

Haby, M.M. et al. Asthma in preschool children: prevalence and risk factors. *Thorax* 2001; 56:589-95.

Oddy, W.H. et al. Maternal asthma, infant feeding, and the risk of asthma in childhood. *J Allergy Clin Immunol* 2002; 110:65-7.

Scariati, P.D. et al. A longitudinal analysis of infant morbidity and the extent of breastfeeding in the United States. *Pediatrics* 1997;99(6):e5.

HIGHER IQS LAST INTO EARLY ADULTHOOD

Studies show differences of five to 10 IQ points between children breastfed as babies and children who were formula-fed. The Mortensen study cited below compared a variety of studies on intelligence, adjusting for the effects of other possible factors such as parents' level of education, mothers' smoking, and infant birth weight. Recent discoveries about docosohexanoic acid (DHA) and arachidonic acid (AA), both of which occur naturally in human milk, and the role they play in the development of the infant's brain provide clues to one possible cause of this difference.

Mortensen, E.L. et al. The association between duration of breastfeeding and adult intelligence. *JAMA* 2002; 28(15):2365-71.

Xiang, M. et al. Long-chain polyunsaturated fatty acids in human milk and brain growth during early infancy. *Acta Paediatr* 2000;89(2):142-47.

DEVELOPS BABIES' IMMUNE SYSTEMS

Human milk contains immunoglobulins, leukocytes and anti-inflammatory factors that help a baby's immune system to mature after birth. The milk produced in the first few days after birth contains especially high concentrations of immune factors. Secretory immunoglobulin A(IgA), one of the live molecules present in human milk, reduces the risk of acute gastrointestinal illnesses in breastfed babies. The IgA present in human milk also stimulates the baby's immunological system to produce more SIgA. Human milk's effects on the baby's immunological system continue to protect the child even after weaning.

Feist, N. et al. Anti-endotoxin antibodies in human milk: Correlation withinfection of the newborn. *Acta Paediatr 2000*; 89(9):1087-92.

Mackie, R.I. et al. Developmental microbial ecology of the neonatal gastrointestinal tract. *Am J Clin Nutr* 1999; 69(Suppl):1035S-45S.

Ronayne de Ferrer, P.A. et al. Lactoferrin levels in term and preterm milk. J Am Coll Nutr 2000; 19(3):370-73.

THE ENVIRONMENT BENEFITS

Breastfeeding uses none of the metal, paper, plastic, or energy necessary for preparing, packaging, and transporting artificial baby milks and feeding devices. Since human milk is more fully utilized by the baby, each breastfed baby cuts down on pollution and waste disposal problems. In addition, research shows that exclusive breastfeeding naturally spaces pregnancies. Although we live in a polluted world, scientists agree that human milk is still the very best food to nourish human babies, and it may even protect babies from some of the effects of pollution.

Lovelady, C.A. et al. Weight change during lactation does not alter the concentrations of chlorinated organic contaminants in breast milk of women with low exposure. *J Hum Lact* 1999: 15(4):307-15.

ESTABLISHING YOUR MILK SUPPLY

A baby's need for milk and his mother's ability to produce it in just the right quantity have been said to be one of nature's most perfect examples of the law of supply and demand. Until the advent of mass produced artificial formula, the very survival of the human race depended largely on a mother's ability to produce a sufficient quantity of milk to adequately nourish her baby. Establishing and maintaining an ample milk supply is easy when you understand how the milk supply is regulated and what kinds of things are likely to upset the balance between the amount of milk the baby needs and the amount of milk that is produced .

The more the baby nurses, the more milk there will be. This is the key to an abundant milk supply and a contented baby. Milk is produced almost continuously, and the more often the baby nurses, the more milk there will be. Frequent nursing and effective sucking signal the mother's body to produce the amount of milk her baby needs.

Nursing early and often is one of the most important factors in getting breastfeeding off to a good start. Mothers who are permitted to nurse their babies at frequent, unrestricted intervals following birth are more likely to have a good milk supply sooner than mothers who are allowed to nurse only on a restricted feeding schedule.

Newborns usually nurse about every two hours, or at least eight to 12 times per day. This frequent nursing provides a wonderful source of comfort as well as nutrition for the newborn, and helps assure that the mother's milk supply will quickly become well established.

Allow the baby to nurse as long as he seems interested, right from the start. Mothers are sometimes advised to limit nursing to five minutes or less during the first week in order to avoid sore nipples. However, it may take the milk two or three minutes to "let down," or start to flow, especially in the beginning, so limiting nursing to five minutes may mean the feeding is over almost before it has begun. A baby needs to nurse long enough to get the hindmilk, the milk that comes toward the end of a feeding that is rich and creamy and high in calories.

Offer both breasts at each feeding, especially in the early weeks. A newborn should be nursing on each breast at least every two to three hours (except for, perhaps, one longer stretch at night) during the time when the milk supply is becoming established. Nurse him until he seems satisfied on the first breast (at least 10 to 15 minutes), then offer the second breast. Next feeding, reverse the order offering the last-used breast first.

Be sure the baby is sucking effectively. In order to draw the milk out and stimulate the breasts to produce more, the baby needs to have a large mouthful of breast tissue. Hold your baby in a comfortable position at the level of your nipple with his whole body facing you, being sure that he doesn't have to turn his head or strain to hold onto the nipple. Wait for the baby to open his mouth very wide, then pull him in close to your breast with your nipple far back in his mouth. The baby who is a "cliff hanger" and chews on the end of the nipple instead of milking the breast will get less milk for his efforts, with a correspondingly smaller amount of milk being produced for the next feeding. Sore nipples may also be a byproduct of improper positioning at the breast.

Continue to nurse as often as your baby indicates the need. Keep in mind that since human milk is perfectly suited to your baby, it will be digested more rapidly and completely than cow's milk (formula), so your breastfed baby will be ready to eat again sooner than his bottle-fed counterpart. Remember the law of supply and demand that is at work here—the more often the baby nurses, the more milk your body will produce.

If you find that your baby regularly sleeps more than three hours between feedings, he may need to be awakened for feedings at least every two hours during the day until your milk supply is well established.

If the baby begins to nurse less frequently, there will be a corresponding drop in milk production. A mother may find her breasts overfull if the baby nurses less often than usual. Hand-expressing the excess milk will make you more comfortable, should you find yourself in this situation. If nursings continue to be spaced farther and farther apart or if the baby nurses less vigorously or for a shorter period of time at each feeding, the milk supply will diminish. The law of supply and demand also works in reverse: the less often the baby nurses, the less milk there will be.

Growth spurts or frequency days occur from time to time as the baby goes through a period of rapid growth. Allowing him to nurse more often for two or three days will increase your milk supply to meet his needs.

Remember that newborns nurse for many reasons other than hunger. Your baby may be nursing often because he likes the feeling of security of the close body contact that comes with nursing, because he needs to satisfy his sucking need, or because he finds the sound of your heartbeat and the gentleness of your touch a great source of comfort as he adjusts to his new world.

HOW TO KNOW IF YOUR BREASTFED BABY IS GETTING ENOUGH MILK

- Your baby may have only one or two wet diapers during the first day or two after birth. Beginning about the third or fourth day, your baby will increase the number of wet diapers. After that, he should have at least five to six really wet diapers per day.

- Your baby will pass meconium, the greenish -black, tarry first stool, over the first day or two. By the third day, the color will change to a greenish transitional stool. Baby will begin having at least three to five bowel movements a day beginning about the third day after birth. By the fifth day, these will typically be very loose and bright yellow in color. The amount should be at least the size of a US quarter (2.5 cm).

- Your baby may lose up to seven percent of his/her birth weight during the first three or four days. Once your milk supply becomes more plentiful on the third or fourth day, expect your baby to begin gaining weight. He should regain his birth weight by the time he is10 to 14 days old. After that, most breastfed babies gain an average of six ounces (170 grams) per week or a pound and a half (680 grams) a month for the first four months.

- Your baby will breastfeed frequently, often every one-and-a-half to three hours, averaging about eight to 12 times in 24 hours. Frequent breastfeeding in the early days helps to establish a mother's milk supply.

- Some babies "cluster nurse," which means they nurse very often for a few hours and then sleep for several hours. Feedings are not always spaced at regular intervals.

- Follow baby's feeding cues and do not try to schedule feedings. Crying is considered a late hunger cue.

- You know your baby is getting enough milk when you can see that he looks healthy, his color is good, his skin is firm, he is filling out and growing in length and head circumference, and he is alert and active.

IF YOU NEED TO INCREASE YOUR MILK SUPPLY

- **Get help.** If your baby is not gaining well, or if he is losing weight after the first few days, contact someone who is knowledgeable about breastfeeding. Often, a La Leche League Leader or other breastfeeding specialist can help you improve your breastfeeding techniques and quickly resolve the situation. You will also need to be in close touch with your baby's doctor, because in some cases slow weight gain may indicate a serious health problem.

- **Nurse frequently** for as long as your baby will nurse. A sleepy baby may need to be awakened and encouraged to nurse more fre- quently.Frequent breastfeeding helps to establish a plentiful milk supply. The more often the breasts are stimulated, the more milk they will produce.

- **Offer both breasts at each feeding.** This will ensure that your baby gets all the milk available and that both breasts are stimulated frequently. Allow your baby to indicate he is finished on the first breast, then offer the other breast. Do not try to limit the length of feedings.

- **Be sure that baby is positioned correctly and latched on well.** Baby's lips should be on the areola (dark area surrounding the nipple), well behind the nipple. You should be able to hear your baby swallow. If you are not sure baby is sucking well, or if you feel any nipple soreness when baby is nursing, ask your La Leche League Leader or other breastfeeding specialist to help you.

- **Try breast compression to keep your baby interested in nursing.** Squeeze the breast firmly with your thumb on one side and fingers on the other to increase milk flow. Keep squeezing until baby is no longer actively sucking; then release. Rotate fingers around the breast and squeeze again. Then switch to the other breast, using both breasts twice at each feeding. Squeeze firmly but be careful not to cause injury to your breast tissue.

- **Give your baby only human milk.** If your baby has been receiving formula supplements, do not cut these out abruptly. As you improve your breastfeeding techniques, and your milk supply increases, you will be able to gradually reduce the amount of supplement.But you need to watch baby's wet and soiled diapers to be sure he is getting enough milk. Monitor baby's weight gain and stay in touch with your baby's doctor.
- **All your baby's sucking should be at the breast.** If some supplement is necessary temporarily, it can be given by spoon, cup, or with a nursing supplementer, a device used to feed baby additional milk through a small tube while he nurses at the breast.

- **Pay attention to your own need for rest, relaxation, proper diet, and sufficient fluids.** Taking care of yourself will help your milk supply and improve your general sense of well-being.

"There are three reasons for breast-feeding: the milk is always at the right temperature; it comes in attractive containers; and the cat can't get it." - *Irena Chalmers*

STORING MILK

Storing milk in two to four ounce amounts may reduce waste.

Human milk can be stored in:
- Hard-sided plastic or glass containers with well-fitting tops.
- Plastic bags are not good choices. It's easier to contaminate milkbecause the bags are awkward to handle. They also tend to leak, and some types of plastic may destroy nutrients in milk. If you plan to use bags, select thick plastic nurser bags that are specifically designed for freezing human milk.

GUIDELINES FOR STORAGE:
- At room temperature (less than 75°F, 24°C) for up to 4 hours, although the preference is to refrigerate or chill milk right after it's expressed.
- In a refrigerator for 72 hours. You may add small amounts of chilled milk to a single container over the course of a day.
- In a freezer section of a refrigerator/freezer for up to 3 months if the freezer is separate. The freezer compartment must not be located in the refrigerated section. Store the milk away from the door of the freezer and away from the fan of frost-free models.
- In a deep freeze (-20°F or less, -29°C or less) for up to six months.

Thawing and warming milk:

- Thaw milk in its container.
- Thaw overnight in the refrigerator, under lukewarm running tap water, or in a pan of lukewarm water.
- Do not use hot water or a microwave .
- If milk has been frozen and thawed, it can be refrigerated for up to 24 hours. Do not refreeze.
- Discard leftover milk from a feeding after 1 hour.

Air Feeding

The funniest thing happened when my wife, delirious from breast-feeding and getting little sleep. She walked into our bedroom in the middle of the night, cradling the air. Though she thought our baby was still in her arms, he was actually in his crib.

As told by Jon

Burping

BURPING
When those bubbles just won't come out

When a baby drinks milk, she also takes in air. Until she is about five or six months old, she will need help getting this air out. A bottle-fed newborn should to be burped every two to three ounces, (every four-six ounces for older babies).

If you are breast-feeding, burp your baby as you change breasts. If the baby starts to get squirmy while eating, she probably has to burp. Sometimes, she will not take in enough air to warrant a burp. If she doesn't burp after a few minutes, feed her a little more and try again.

For young babies (0-6 months old), it is not a good idea to feed the whole bottle without trying for a burp, as the baby could spit up. Please know that it's normal for some babies to spit up a little, but if the vomiting is projectile (that is, it goes across the room), is green tinged or if the baby is losing weight or coughs and gags while she feeds, call the pediatrician. Spitting up usually stops around six months or when the baby starts to spend more time upright.

TIPS FOR BURPING
- While sitting, cover your shoulder with a cloth diaper or towel. Hold the baby under her tush and lean her against your chest with her head on your shoulder). Gently rub and pat her back until she burps.

- Hold the baby in the same position as above, but stand and pat her back. Sometimes, the change in gravity will bring up the air.

- Hold the baby under her arms vertically. Gently raise and lower her a few times then put her against your shoulder and pat her back. This action should bring on a good burp.

- Sit the baby on your lap, facing out. Hold the burp cloth under her chin while supporting her head. With the other hand, gently pat and rub her back.

The Exorcist (or Too Much Food for a Four-Day-Old Baby)

The baby was crying and although she had just eaten forty-five minutes earlier, nothing would console her. I tried many different things, but it was 3:00 AM and my husband was less than patient and suggested she might still be hungry. The baby took more food and when I picked her up to burp her over my right shoulder, her head was turned towards him. As daddy looked at her, he watched a stream of projectile vomit hit him right in the eye. He then told the baby to stop crying, she was going to need to learn to work things out for herself.

As told by Wendy

"This is an informative and fun book that really puts parents' worries to rest. It is easy to follow and cites real life experiences. Not everyone is as lucky as my brother and I to have such a great mom! However, this book is a great way to share her vast knowledge of childcare."

Lindsay Lipman
Scottsdale, AZ

"This book would have been a great help when I was raising my three daughters. I surely needed it when I babysat for my three granddaughters. It contains a wealth of good-sense information. Very easy to read!

Grandma Flora, grandma of three
Peoria, AZ

Time to Chew

TIME TO CHEW
Baby's First Real Food

There is no nutritional reason to introduce your baby to solid foods until she is four to six months old. If she is doing fine on the bottle or breast, sleeping through the night, and is happy, don't rush the food. Studies have shown that early introduction of solids may contribute to obesity and/or allergies. Discuss this with your pediatrician. Each baby has different needs.

Babies are born with a tongue-thrust reflex. This allows them to draw the nipple into their mouths and push solid food out. This reflex diminishes around four months. When the baby is first getting used to solids, she will stick out her tongue when you put food in her mouth. This is natural and will take a little practice. If she cries, wiggles, and totally rejects solids, she may  not be ready. Don't be stressed, just wait a few weeks and try the solids again. There is no magic age. If a baby is getting hungry an hour after a feeding, and she wakes up many times during the night after the first two months, it might be time to start cereal. Check with your pediatrician before starting any solid food.

Never force your baby to eat. Eating should be a fun adventure, not a battleground.

When the time does come, have the camera ready to roll, the faces will be indescribable!

CEREAL

Mix two tablespoons of rice cereal with formula or breast milk. (If you use water, you'll miss out on those vitamins and nutrients.) Make the consistency like runny soup for the first few feedings, but not as thin as formula. Here are some tips on feeding.

- Put a little onto an infant spoon and place it into the baby's mouth leaving the spoon in for a few seconds so she can suck the cereal off and get used to the consistency. Do this for the first few feedings. Be ready, most of it will come out. Just put it back in if she likes it. As your baby gets used to it, gradually make the cereal a little thicker for each feeding until it is the consistency of creamy oatmeal (not thick though).

- Put the spoon in the baby's mouth sideways, this keeps most of the food from coming back out.

- Another technique is using your finger as baby's first spoon. Wash your hands. Dip your finger into the cereal. Place a few drops onto her lips, then some on the tip of her tongue. When she swallows this, put some onto the middle of her tongue and let her practice. Try this for a few feedings, if she likes it, and then graduate to a spoon.

- Make sure your baby is in an upright position when feeding. You might want to start with her in the infant seat and then later graduate to the high chair. You may also hold the baby in the crook of your arm, but it's hard to juggle the baby, the spoon, and a bowl of food.

- If you want to keep your baby from putting her hands into her mouth while feeding in the infant seat, give her something to hold, or put her hands under the fabric that goes across her tummy when you buckle her in.

- If you are feeding her in the high chair and the food is going everywhere but in her mouth, give her something to hold, (a toy, a spoon, a plastic bowl, or a toy with a suction cup on the bottom that will stick to the high chair). Do not put the baby into a high chair until she can sit up. Some high chairs recline, which is ideal for the baby that is not yet ready to sit up.

- Another method to keep her from rubbing the food all over is to put her hands on her lap and push the high chair tray in loosely. This may look like a straitjacket, but makes feeding easier, as long as she doesn't protest.

- It's very hard for a baby to just sit still and eat. A great distraction is for you to sing and even do a little dance. Think of it as Dinner Theater! Babies love to be entertained and love to laugh. Even though the food may still be all over, a floor show could make you both happier.

- Many pediatricians recommend introducing vegetables after cereal and then introducing fruit last. If you start with fruit, some babies will not eat the vegetables after enjoying the sweet taste of fruit. Always introduce one food at a time and do it for four consecutive days. This allows any food allergies to present themselves.

FIRST FOODS LIST
Cereal:
1. Rice, without added fruit. (Most pediatricians do not recommend starting mixed cereals until the baby is six months old and has been introduced to the other food groups.)
2. Oatmeal, Barley. (If the baby is doing well on rice cereal, you do not have to try the others)

Vegetables and Meat:
1. Squash, carrots, or sweet potatoes
2. Green beans, peas, spinach, corn, potatoes
3. Chicken, beef

Fruit:
1. Applesauce, bananas, pears
2. Peaches, apricots, plums, prunes (just a little)
3. Mixed fruits such as apple/strawberry, apple/mango, blueberry/ banana pear/blueberry, tropical fruit blend, etc.
4. Yogurt, vanilla custard pudding (baby food brand)

SECOND STAGE FOODS

You can introduce any of the Stage Two foods and combinations after the baby has been on the above single foods and is doing well (without any rashes, coughs, or any type of allergic reaction). Always contact your pediatrician if you feel she is having some type of allergic reaction (rash, congestion, loose stools, gas) and stop the food immediately.

THIRD STAGE FOODS

These are combination foods with some texture and small pieces to practice chewing. Most grocery stores carry all the stages.

You may prefer to make your baby food. Steam vegetables and put them into the blender to puree. You may also puree any type of meat. If it is too thick, add a little formula or breast milk until you get the desired consistency. Be careful with spices, as babies' tummies can be sensitive and not ready for that garlic flavor we all love.

FINGER FOODS

Start with tiny pieces on the high chair tray, letting your baby pick them up (this is good practice for small-motor coordination). Never leave the baby unsupervised when she is eating any food. Try the following, one at a time.

1. Some snacks that melt easily in baby's mouth when she only has a few teeth:

• Cheerios	• Rice cakes
• Arrowroot cookies	• Rice puffed cereal
• Graham Crackers or sticks	• Pirates Booty Snacks
• Cheese curls	

2. Snacks that are a little harder to chew:

• Animal Crackers	• Apple
• Goldfish crackers	• Cantaloupe
• Goldfish pretzels	• Watermelon
• Nutri-Grain® bars	• Honeydew
• Oatmeal bars	• Peeled grapes
• Banana	

3. Breakfast, lunch and dinner ideas when baby food is not interesting anymore (check with your pediatrician about adding dairy foods if your baby is still drinking formula)

• French toast	• Matzo ball soup
• French toast sticks	• Yogurt
• Pancakes	• Cottage cheese
• Toast with jam	• Cheese
• Waffles	• Turkey
• Turkey sausage (skinned)	• Ham
• Eggs (check with pediatrician first)	• Chicken
	• Cheese
• Spaghetti	• Macaroni and cheese
• Pasta with butter or tomato sauce	• Vegetable soup
	• Pizza
• Lasagna	• Rice
• Broccoli with cheese	• Baked potato

It's always a good idea to check with your pediatrician before introducing a new food that is not on your list. Here are a few foods to avoid with babies under one year.

DAIRY PRODUCTS	SPICY FOODS
• Yogurt	• Onions
• Cottage cheese	• Chilies
• Cheese	• Fried or fatty foods
• Eggs	• Nuts
• Citrus fruits	• Nut products
• Honey	• Peanut butter
	• Hot dogs

The Sippy Cup

When the baby is about six months and eating all of her meals in the high chair, you can introduce liquids in a sippy cup, which is a cup with a cover and spout. There are many types. I like the one that has two handles, as it makes it easy for the baby to hold and drink without dropping the cup.

Put water into the cup and offer it with each meal or snack. Show the baby how to hold the cup. After a few times just set it on the high chair and encourage her to try it with each meal when she is thirsty or anytime during the day. Take the cup with you when you go out, as it's always important to have water available. If you avoid putting sugary drinks in the cup, she will get into the habit of drinking water when she is thirsty. You may use fruit juice as a treat, but it's not necessary if she is getting her fruit at mealtimes. Fruit juice has lots of sugar so when I gave my children fruit juice, I always mixed 3/4 water to 1/4 fruit juice.

If your baby has a hard time with the sippy cup, offer her a prepackaged water bottle. Let her suck on the spout as she will think this is cool, and it will get her used to something other than the nipple.

Put water into a cup with a straw. Hold the straw and the cup for her and see what happens. Some babies love drinking this way.

As she gets the hang of it, start putting her formula into the cup at meals. Don't use this instead of the bottle until she drinks at least six ounces from the cup.

"More Help! My Baby Came Without Instructions! *is a practical, common sense approach to dealing with issues parents of newborns face. Blythe's grandmotherly wisdom will be put to good use by this generation of parents without direct access to grandmothers. I recommend it to all new parents.*"

Ronald S. Fischler, MD Pediatrician
Scottsdale, AZ

"I wish I'd had this book available twenty years ago when I had my two baby girls. They did not sleep for the first year and a half, and now I need plastic surgery for the bags under my eyes that never went away! Every new mother needs this book to survive the first few years of their children's lives."

Kathy Arak, mother of two
Scottsdale, AZ

Ouch!
My Gums Are Killing Me!

OUCH! MY GUMS ARE KILLING ME

How to Help Baby Through the Teething Stage

Teething is tough for baby, *and* for mommy and daddy. It can start weeks or months before the baby's first teeth appear. Teething is usually full-blown around seven months. She may have one or more of the following symptoms or none at all.

- clear runny nose
- diaper rash
- excessive drooling (which may cause a red, itchy rash around the mouth
- crankiness
- refuses solids
- cries when sucking on a bottle
- chews on everything, including her fingers
- swollen, red gums
- wakes up crying from a sound sleep
- loose stools (because an excess of saliva is swallowed)

Teething *does not* cause fever or colds. The baby's resistance may be lowered while teething, as she is not sleeping as well and you may see a cold or viral infection. Just do your best to get her to stick to her regular sleeping schedule, allowing her immune system to stay strong while those teeth are being born.

TIPS TO MAKE HER FEEL BETTER

- Frozen bagels to gnaw on

- Frozen, white washcloth (make sure there is no soap residue)

- A frozen banana

- Teething rings that have been frozen or cooled in the refrigerator

- Fruit juice Popsicle®

- Cold drinks such as juice, water, or formula

- Fill a clean, white, cotton athletic sock with ice, tie a knot in the end. Put the baby in the high chair or Exersaucer® (see *Glossary*) and let her gnaw away.

- Teething biscuits (watch her carefully, as large pieces of the biscuit can break off)

- Baby Orajel® Homeopathic teething tablets, gel or liquid by Hyland® or Humphreys®

- A dose of liquid, infant acetaminophen (but only as recommended by a pediatrician) will relieve pain for a few hours. When we have a headache, we don't think twice about taking something for the pain. Babies are no different, they feel pain just as we do.

- Wrap a clean piece of gauze around your finger and gently massage the baby's gums.

- Put the baby into her high chair and give her some ice cubes to gnaw on and play with, this feels good, is lots of fun and numbs the gums.

Remember, anytime you give your baby any type of food, make sure you do not leave her unattended, *not even for one second!*

A baby is a blank check made payable
to the human race.

"Blythe Lipman has written a "how to" handbook that no first time parent should be without. In her own style, she has accomplished an easy and humorous format. A primer that guides you and dispels any doubt a new parent may have. It will probably save countless calls to the pediatrician or that other expert, Mom. No new parent should be without it."

Dr. Stephen M. Grunfeld D.C.
Scottsdale, AZ

"This is a concise, yet comprehensive reference guide written with a sense of humor."

Lisa Kitty, favorite Aunt
Ashland, MA

My Baby Walked at Six Months, How About Yours?

MY BABY WALKED AT SIX MONTHS, HOW ABOUT YOURS?
Bragging and Other Nonsense

Friends, neighbors, grandparents, godparents, aunts, uncles, and cousins. Then there are all those books. Books, books, and more books. It seems everyone is an authority on babies, including *your* baby. They all "know" when the baby should sit up, when they should begin eating cereal, sleeping through the night, when they first smile, coo, etc., etc., etc.

It's so difficult *not* to compare your baby's progress and growth to your friends' babies and all the advice bombarding you. The truth is (and you already know this, it's just hard to remember) that each baby is different. They do all these things when they are ready and not one minute before (even if Aunt Tillie's son *did* get his teeth when he was three months old!) As long as your baby is healthy and full of smiles, relax and enjoy each minute with your new bundle of joy.

But when you do start to compare (and it's inevitable, at times), here are some important things for you to remember and do:

- Simply watch your baby smile.

- Enjoy looking at your baby sleeping peacefully.

- Sing a song and play with her.

- Look in the mirror and see *your* happiness.

- If a "comparison braggart" calls on the phone, politely end the conversation, hang up, and then do the first four things on this list.

- If, however, you are at the mall with your baby and a "comparison braggart" comes along, you might want to pretend your cell phone is ringing and excuse yourself and walk away.

- If you are talking to Grandma or any other relative on the phone, and comparisons are making your phone line sizzle, say, "I am sorry, but someone is at the door."

- If you still wonder if your baby is lagging a bit behind in some area of development, put both you and your baby in front of a mirror and enjoy the beautiful sight.

- If daddy starts comparing, take him, the baby, and yourself to a mirror. Have a group hug and marvel at this great miracle that is yours.

Cone Head

Daddies sometimes have no ideas about what the baby may look like when he or she is born. They picture the Gerber baby! My husband had no idea that the head of a baby is sometimes cone-shaped when the baby is born. Even though he didn't say anything at the delivery, my husband later told me he was very scared and thought to himself, "She is so beautiful, but what happened to her head?" Poor guy.

As told by Alice

**The joy of having a baby today can only be expressed
in two words: tax deduction.**

"Your book is a wonderful creation with great tips for new mothers and fathers. It was a real pleasure to read, quick and entertaining."
Nancy Roepke, Ph.D., Family Counselor
Scottsdale, AZ

"Must-know bits of information for those maternal "that didn't work so what do I do now" moments. I consider this essential reading for all new mothers."

Konrad Kail, P.A., N.D.
Phoenix, AZ

Daddy Loves Me

DADDY LOVES ME
The Manly Art of Baby Care

There's nothing like daddies and their babies. Fathers love to be involved with their babies. They do everything—diapering, feeding, bathing, and their favorite, playing.

Here are a few tips for daddy. Pass them on gently.

- When changing the baby's diaper, make sure to have everything you need (diaper, wipes, ointment, etc.) before you lay the baby down. Take the diaper off and don't let the baby lie there naked for long, as they love to pee when they are naked! (Note of caution: little boys pee up, so watch your face.) Pull the  diaper up between the legs and attach the tape on each side, being sure not to make the diaper too tight or too loose. If you can get your finger easily into the top near her tummy, it's too loose. If you can't get your finger in at all, it's too tight. Pull out the elastic between her legs as it can pinch. Now take the baby and the grin on your face and enjoy.

- When changing a diaper, always give the baby something to hold. Those little hands are faster than you think and you don't want them grabbing the you-know-what.

- Don't be afraid to hold your tiny baby. Pretend you are gently cradling a football. Babies love to be held close to your heart. The sound of your heart beating is very comforting, and your strong, gentle hands make her feel even more secure.

- Don't be afraid to act silly. Sing songs, play games, dance, make sounds, etc. The sillier the better. Your baby will love it.

- If you have carpool duty, *don't* take your sick baby to preschool, or to the baby-sitter with Tylenol under her belt, even if you think she has only a tiny fever. You will get that dreaded phone call four hours later when it wears off. Save yourself the aggravation of having to leave work or a fight with your wife. Keep the baby home, if you think she is sick.

NO INSTRUCTIONS INCLUDED

- If you're not sure what to do in a situation with the baby (feeding, burping, sleeping, etc.), don't be afraid to ask. Babies **don't** come with instructions.

Dining With Daddy

Mommy was busy at work and daddy had to pick our baby girl Jordan up from day care. He left work, very excited to take his eight-month-old daughter out to lunch at a Mexican fast-food restaurant.

Day care gave daddy a diaper, a *few* wipes, and a bottle to take with him. Well, Jordan was in the stroller while daddy was eating when daddy thought he smelled something. Yuck, dirty diaper. He looked in the restroom to see if there was a changing table. No such luck. He would have to change her in the stroller. Daddies don't always know that you need to give the baby something to hold while changing them. Uh-oh. Jordan put her hands in the dirty diaper and smeared it all over and daddy didn't have many wipes. He had to take her in the restroom, put her in the sink and clean her up. Poor Daddy!

This was so embarrassing, but it doesn't end here. While he was driving home, he called mommy at work to tell her his tale of woe. Mommy was a little busy and to make it easier, put him on speaker-phone. You guessed it, the whole office heard his terrible tale.

So, two lessons to be learned. Always have an extra box of wipes in your car and always ask if you are on speaker phone!

As told by Randy

Giving birth is like taking your lower lip and forcing it over your head!

I always wondered why babies spend so much time
sucking their thumbs.
Then I tasted BABY FOOD!

I Love You But I'm So Tired

I LOVE YOU BUT I'M SO TIRED
Balancing It All

Here she is, the most adorable, lovable, cuddly baby. She demands your attention almost 24 hours a day. You love your new baby and your new job, but you are so tired.

Here he is, the most adorable, lovable, cuddly husband. He needs your time, attention and love, but you are so tired!

Here she is, the most adorable, lovable, cuddly wife. She needs your time, attention and TLC, but you have to go to work and you are so tired!

Having a new baby brings on so many demands, and it seems as if there are never enough hours in the day and certainly not enough energy for anything but baby care. Here are a few tips to make sure you don't forget you were once a couple in love and should always stay that way.

1) When you are at the drugstore, card store, or variety store, stock up on those special romance greeting cards. Once a week or at least once every two weeks, write a loving message in a card and put it someplace special for your honey to find. Even put it in a funny place (i.e. where you keep the breast pump, bottle nipples, in a shoe, etc.), making it not only loving, but fun.

2) Order flowers to be sent to your honey once a month. Prepay for three months and make out three cards to be sent with them. You can send them more often if you wish. Keep that romance alive. (Daddy, this one is for you!)

3) Have food delivered to your honey at work. But call first, to make sure there are no lunch meetings scheduled.

4) While the baby is sleeping, set the table with a tablecloth, candles, cloth napkins, and your best paper plates. Ask your honey to pick up Chinese food on the way home. Turn the lights down, light the candles, put on some music and enjoy each other (even if you are still in your "baby care" clothes).

5) Ask grandma to take the baby. Surprise your honey with a special night for two. You can:
   a) Go out to dinner at a favorite restaurant.
   b) Get take-out from a favorite restaurant.
   c) Go to the movies.
   d) Rent a movie and make popcorn.
   e) Read the paper together or take a long walk.
   f) Go out with friends.
   g) Go to the mall and buy each other a special present for being new parents.
   h) Go to a club and listen to music.

i) Go dancing.
j) Go to the ice cream shop and share a banana split (calcium is good for the baby if you are nursing!).
k) Take a picnic to the park.
l) Go to the bookstore and buy a book that is not about babies.
m) Just cuddle until you both fall asleep—for the **Entire Night!**

Show and Tell

I've been teaching now for about fifteen years. I have two kids myself, but the best birth story I know is the one I saw in my second grade classroom a few years back. It was an Oscar-worthy performance.

When I was a kid, I loved show-and-tell. So, I always have a few sessions with my students. It always helps them get over shyness and experience a little public speaking. And it gives me a break and some guaranteed entertainment!

Usually show-and-tell is pretty tame. Kids bring in pet turtles, model airplanes, pictures of fish they catch, stuff like that. And I never place any boundaries or limitations on them. If they want to lug it to school and talk about it, they're welcome.

Well, one day this little girl, Erica, a very bright, very outgoing kid, takes her turn and waddles up to the front of the class with a pillow stuffed under her sweater. She holds up a snapshot of an infant. "This is Luke, my baby brother, and I'm going to tell you about his birthday. First, Mommy and Daddy made him as a symbol of their love, and then Daddy put a seed in my mother's stomach and Luke grew in there. He ate for nine months through an umbrella cord."

She's standing there with her hands on the pillow, and I'm trying not to laugh wishing I had a video camera rolling. The kids are watching her in amazement.

"Then, about two Saturdays ago, my mother starts going, 'Oh, oh, oh!'" Erica puts a hand behind her back and groans. "She walked around the house for like an hour saying, "Oh, oh, oh!"

Now the kids' are doing this hysterical duck-walk, holding their backs and groaning.

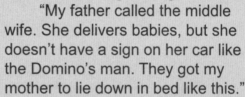

"My father called the middle wife. She delivers babies, but she doesn't have a sign on her car like the Domino's man. They got my mother to lie down in bed like this."

Erica lies down with her back against the wall. "And then, pop! My mother had this bag of water she kept in there in case he got thirsty, and it just blew up and spilled all over the bed, like psshheew!"

The kid has her legs spread and with her little hands is miming water flowing away. It was too much!

"Then the middle wife starts going push, push, and breathe, breathe. They start counting, but they never even got past ten. Then, all of a sudden, out comes my brother. He was covered in yucky stuff they said was from the play-center, so there must be a lot of stuff inside there!"

Then Erica stood up. Took a big theatrical bow and returned to her seat. I'm sure I applauded the loudest. Ever since then, if it's show-and-tell day, I bring my camcorder, just in case another Erica comes along!

Told by Betsey

The Taking Care Of Me MANUAL

I'm a New Mom and Don't Know What to Do!

I'm a New Mom and Don't Know What to Do!
Survival 101 — Learning How to Take Care of Yourself

Okay, so you haven't taken a shower in two days. Make-up? What's that? Your shirt is adorned with spit-up, grandma went home, and now you're all alone with your baby. You have never been so tired in all your life. Still, when your baby looks up and smiles, your heart just melts.

Here are some survival tips to make your transition to "real-time mom" a little more manageable:

* IMPORTANT – Don't forget to eat. You need your energy to take good care of your baby. Without fuel your car just won't run!

* Try to stock up on healthy foods, soups, frozen gourmet meals, baked chicken, etc. If you have good food at your fingertips, chances are you will take better care of yourself.

* Plan a trip to the grocery store once a week (without the baby, if possible). Buy lots of healthy fruits and vegetables. Wash them and put them in a bowl in the refrigerator to have handy when that energy drain hits.

* If you can't get to the grocery store alone, pick a time when you know the baby won't need a feeding.

* When you go to the grocery store, buy yourself a special treat.

A candy bar, gossip magazine, special food, something that is just a little indulgent and will make you feel good about taking care of yourself as well as your baby. A little self-pampering never hurt anyone.

- Even though you always did your own laundry, cleaned your own house, and mowed your own lawn, don't feel guilty about hiring a professional to help those first few months. Sometimes you can't do it all, and that's perfectly fine.

- Place bottled water around the house just for **you**. It is very important to drink lots of fluids, especially if you are nursing. There is nothing more frustrating than sitting down to feed your baby and remembering you haven't had anything to drink in hours.

- It's a fact of life that you are going to be up all hours of the night feeding the baby (she doesn't know what time it is). Try to make it fun. Turn on a comedy channel or rent some funny movies. There is nothing better than a good laugh to help you forget your fatigue.

- While everyone is very excited about meeting your new little bundle, don't be afraid to say, "Thank you but please, no visitors today." Wait until you are ready to handle more than just you and your baby. Waiting a week or two for the introduction won't matter a bit. Say, "I can't wait for you to meet Lindsay, but today just won't work. I will call you soon, I promise." Above all, don't feel guilty about it. You are not obligated to anyone except yourself, your baby, and your husband.

- While Grandma means well and wants to be there to help you every second, it's smart to establish some ground rules for visiting and hanging out from the very beginning. It will help ease any hard feelings that may otherwise come up. Be nice and let her know you understand how excited she is, but you need some time to ease into your new routine.

- If the Grandma in question happens to be your mother-in-law, ask your husband to talk to her. Sometimes a child has a better way of getting mom to understand since he lived with her his whole life.

- Remember these words: "Yes, thank you so much. You're such a great friend!" These are the words to use when a friend asks you if they can pick up your dry cleaning, get you a few things at the grocery store, and return your movies. If someone offers to help, throw away your "Super Mom" costume and take them up on it. True friends help each other. Besides, you know you'd do the same for them.

- Lastly, sometimes a good cry is all you need. Give into those tears. Transitioning into motherhood isn't easy. Get out the tissue box, and let those tears flow. I promise, you will feel better soon.

"One of the most important things to remember is never to change diapers in mid-stream."

I Really Need a Break!

I Really Need a Break!

How to Create the Perfect Caregiver

Your baby is a month old and she sleeping only three, maybe four hours at a crack. You're not only feeling really good about being a mother, you're feeling great! But you'd still love to have a break from all the responsibility and work—maybe get your hair cut, go to the bookstore, go out with your husband, or just meet a friend for coffee.

I know, you're worried whether you'd relax enough to take that much-needed time to be an adult.

While the most wonderful thing in the whole world is being a new mommy, being a woman and an independent adult is just as important. Why? Because taking care of yourself and balancing your life and responsibilities are critical components to be being a truly great mom.

Leaving your baby with someone can be one of the scariest things a new mother faces. You think of every possible scenario that could go wrong. My baby won't eat. She won't sleep. She'll fall off the changing table. The house will catch on fire. Some are well-founded, but others arise out of pure fear. While all these thoughts are normal, it's important to put things in perspective. If you pick a caregiver you're comfortable with and one you know will give your baby the best possible care, then take a deep breath, pick up your purse, and go have some fun!

Here are just a few pointers to have you breathing more easily:

- Caregivers come in lots of shapes and sizes. You can hire a teenager, go to a professional nanny agency, or maybe you can rely on your extended family. The most important thing to remember is to choose someone that makes **you** feel totally comfortable. A person you know that will follow your instructions, someone who's had experience caring for infants.

- Give very clear *written* instructions. If your baby is on a schedule, write down the times she has been eating, sleeping, etc., and ask your caregiver is she has any questions.

- Leave your caregiver some paper and a pen to record the times your baby eats, sleeps, or has a soiled diaper.

- While it is nice to have your baby on a schedule, make sure to leave some wiggle room if she decides to do something totally different today. As long as your baby eats, sleeps, and is happy, it really doesn't matter. Formula tastes just as good at eleven o'clock as it does at ten.

- Make sure to tell your caregiver what **you** do when the baby cries. Tell her if the baby likes the swing, bouncy seat, or stroller. Leave a copy of my book (*More Help! My Baby Came Without Instructions*) on the counter!

- Tell your caregiver what your baby **doesn't** like. Some babies hate to be swaddled, even if this always worked for her babies.

- Don't forget to show her where you keep everything: clothes, diapers, burp cloths, etc. Or if it makes you feel better, lay out an extra set of clothes, burp cloths, some diapers, and wipes to make it easier.

- Show your caregiver where the phones and the emergency numbers are located in your house.

- Clearly communicate your wishes. Tell your caregiver that it is okay if your baby doesn't drink the entire bottle or she can have extra formula if she needs more. Leaving choices up to her is sometimes upsetting to you because they may be different than yours.

- If Grandma is the caregiver, try cutting her some slack and not getting defensive when she starts giving you unsolicited advice. She's just trying to help. Tell her she has great ideas, but your baby is happiest following your schedule.

- If Daddy is watching the baby for the first time alone, be clear and **gentle**. He wants to make you and the baby happy and not mess up! Have the schedule written down for him. The more details you give him, the better he will feel. It's scary to be in charge of this tiny baby.

- Leave your phone numbers in clear view, just in case.

- Try and restrain yourself from calling more than once. I know it's difficult, but if your caregiver needs you, she will call.

- If you are running late, do call. But chances are the first time out you will be out of breath from rushing to get home early!

- If you arrive home and the baby is crying, try not to get upset and jump to conclusions. Nicely ask what is wrong. Remember, your baby sometimes cries when you take care of her, too.

- While the connection between you and your baby may be the most glowing bond in your life. It is important as she gets older to expose her to other caregivers beside yourself. It is important for her to learn to trust other people, a skill that will help promote confidence and independence as she blossoms and grows.

So are you ready? Good! Take a deep breath, put on those dancing shoes, give your baby a kiss, and walk out the door with that glowing new mom expression knowing that you are taking care of yourself and your baby is in good hands.

**People who say they sleep like babies
obviously don't have any!**

A New Baby, the Perfect Present!

A New Baby, the Perfect Present!
Holiday Celebrations Made Easier

Holidays are a great time to share joy and welcome a new baby. But with all the hustle and bustle, this time of year can be more than a little unnerving for new parents. What do you do when all the relatives want to meet and greet your new little bundle? You watch in stunned silence as they pass her around like a football and kiss her little face. And what do you do when it's time for that holiday dinner and your little sweetie thinks it's time for a cry?

So many questions, but where are the answers? Here are some tips to make the holidays full of happiness and good cheer:

- If you are traveling by plane, it's a good idea to feed your baby while the plane is taking off and landing. This will help keep the eustachian tubes open so her ears won't hurt.

- Remember to take a change of clothes for yourself on the plane, too. There's nothing worse than meeting the family wearing strained carrots even if orange is your favorite color!

- If you are staying in a hotel, bring along the lullaby CD that you play for your baby at home. Most hotels have CD players or you can request one. Both you and your baby will enjoy the comforting sounds of home.

- Call ahead and see how many people are going to be at the gathering. If it is not going to be comfortable for you and your baby, you have the right to choose not to go.

- Before leaving home for that visit to a relative's house, you and your husband should agree on a time limit for your stay. Have a signal between the two of you so you'll both know when it's time to make a graceful exit

- If you are going to be at the gathering for any length of time, make sure your baby is dressed in a comfortable outfit.Those frilly dresses with matching headbands and miniature Doc Martens look adorable. But after awhile, they can get hot and itchy.

- If your baby is on a napping schedule, plan the visit for after naptime. There is nothing worse than Aunt Fannie trying to hold and play with a tired, cranky baby.

- Try to feed your baby before arriving for a holiday visit. A full tummy makes a happy baby.

- If you are having the holiday celebration at your home, hire a caregiver to help you with the baby. Or hire a caterer to help you with the food and festivities. Don't be afraid to ask for help. You don't need to be Superwoman!

- If you don't want your baby passed around, put her in the bouncy seat or stroller.

- If your baby starts to cry while Aunt Judy is holding her, gently take her. Try not to get upset or the baby will sense your tension and continue to cry.

- If you arrive at the celebration and your baby starts crying, immediately take her outside to calm her down. Even though well-meaning relatives think they know how to do it better, there is nothing more comforting than mommy or daddy's arms.

The holidays are a time for sharing. These tips will help you and your new family create wonderful celebrations full of smiles, laughter, great memories, and love.

A baby will make love stronger, days shorter, nights longer, bankroll smaller, home happier, clothes shabbier, the past forgotten, and the future worth living for.

Whenever I held my newborn baby in my arms, I used to think that what I said and did to him could have an influence not only on him but on all whom he met, not only for a day or a month or a year, but for all eternity - a very challenging and exciting thought for a mother.
~Rose Kennedy

The Fine Art of Baby-Proofing Your Home

The Fine Art of Baby-Proofing Your Home
How to Keep Your Baby Safe

Before you know it, your baby will be sitting up by herself, and next she'll be rocking on her knees figuring out how to crawl. It's just about the cutest thing she's ever done. And it all happens so fast!

So there you are on the floor admiring her newly-acquired talents. You look over at the wall and notice the computer cord hanging there, the uncovered electric outlets on every wall, and for the first time you realize how sharp edges of the coffee table are. Until now, you'd never realized your house was such a danger zone.

It's time to take action—before your baby starts crawling across the floor at breakneck speed. Get down on the floor, crawl around, and see the things she sees from her level.

Tasting, touching, and feeling are how infants and toddlers learn about the amazing world around them. Therefore, you'll want to make sure they do their exploring in an environment that's as safe as possible. The following tips will help make your home a safe place for your baby to blossom and grow.

- Cover all electrical outlets.

- Place any hanging or loose cords from computers, lamps, phones, etc. well out of your baby's reach.

- However, don't use tacks or staples to secure these cords to the wall, as they can fall out and end up in your baby's mouth.

- If you have a computer, make sure the safety strip is not sitting on the floor. Hang it on a wall, lay it on the desk, or make that room off limits.

- Get toilet locks so your toilet lids stay down. Tragically, babies have drowned by pulling themselves up on the toilet and falling in. As a double safety measure, always keep your bathroom door closed.

- Cover the tub faucet with a soft rubber cover to prevent your baby from clunking her head on the hard metal. Many stores sell them in fun animal shapes.

- Install childproof latches on all kitchen, bathroom, and bedroom cabinets your baby can reach.

- Regardless of childproof latches, **ALWAYS** keep your cleaning supplies in high cabinets completely beyond the reach of your toddler.

- **ALWAYS** keep all of your medicines locked up in a high cabinet.

- Never keep your vitamins or baby's medicine on the kitchen counter. From the very beginning, get in the habit of keeping these things out of reach.

- Buy trash cans with covers and keep the trash cans under the sinks behind the locked cabinet doors.

- Get covers for your stove knobs that will prevent your toddler from being able to turn on the stove.

- Get cover guards for all tables with sharp edges.

- A glass table can break if a baby climbs on it. Remove the table or replace it with Plexiglas.

- If you have a fireplace, purchase a hearth cover or a piece of soft foam and soft foam edging to prevent your toddler from hitting her head.

- Remove the gas jet key if you have a gas fireplace.Use a fireplace door guard to secure the fireplace screen doors.

- Make sure your child can't open the doors to your entertainment wall unit.

- Secure all bookshelves to the wall so your baby can't pull them over. Also, it's a good idea to place the heavier items on the bottom shelves.

- Make sure to secure anything that the baby could possibly pull over.

- Check to see that the carpeting doesn't have any sharp tacks sticking out.

- Get a TV guard that covers all the controls.

- Don't put televisions, microwaves, fish tanks or other appliances on carts with wheels that your toddler can push.

- Take your bottles of wine out of the wine racks and store them in a place your baby can't reach.

- Make sure the cords from your blinds are out of your baby's reach.

- If you save your change, keep the container in a high place. Babies love to put money in their mouths.

- Clear all surfaces at or below the level of your chest.

- Use mesh gates to block off certain unsafe rooms and the stairs.

- Put slip-proof mats under throw rugs and door mats so your toddler won't fall.

- Get doorknob covers to prevent your toddler from opening the doors.

- Drape a cloth diaper or washcloth over the tops of doors your baby can push closed to prevent pinching her little fingers.

- If you have door stoppers with rubber tips, take the tips off or install the kind that come in one solid piece. Those rubber tips become a terrible choking hazard if they go into your baby's mouth.

- Install a deadbolt or chain on the top of your exterior doors so your baby cannot open them.

- If you have a pool, put an alarm on all your doors leading outside, even if it has a fence around it. You can *never* be too safe with a pool.

- You should also purchase a pool alarm that alerts you if anyone or anything falls in.

- Install window guards on all your windows that can be opened. Use guards that can be easily removed in case of an emergency. Never nail shut a window.

- Keep all houseplants our of your toddler's reach. If you own any poisonous plants, pitch them.

- Buy a bottle of ipecac syrup, just in case. But do not use it until you have spoken to poison control or a physician. The phone number for the National Poison Hotline is: 1-800-222-1222. Put this important number on your refrigerator for a fast reference.

- If you have any unused appliances (refrigerators, washers, dryers, etc.), make sure the doors are locked (or removed) so your toddler can't climb in to play.

- Store your purse out of reach.

- Keep your pet's food out of your baby's reach.

- Keep a stocked and up-to-date first-aid kit within reach as well as all your emergency numbers posted in clear view. (Not in a phone book in the drawer)

  This list should contain everything you need to know to make your home safe. Remember, if your toddler is not supposed to have it, she will definitely want it. Make it easy on yourself and safe for her—just remove it.

Ten tiny little fingers that always want to play,
That never stop exploring the wonder of today.
Ten tiny little fingers that from the very start,
Will reach out for tomorrow yet always hold your heart.

Yikes, is it Time to Go Back to Work Already?

Yikes, is it Time to Go Back to Work Already?

Choosing the Perfect Preschool for your Infant

Finding the perfect preschool for your infant is one of the most important things any new parent needs to accomplish. Not only does the infant care have to be the best, but all aspects of the school have to make you feel comfortable. When you drop off your baby each morning, you want to leave feeling comfortable that your baby will be receiving the love, nurturing and care she needs.

When checking out a preschool, the following questions should help make your decision easier. I suggest you fill this out while you're there instead of relying on your memory.

Preschool Interview Checklist

- When you call for an appointment, did the director speak to you?

- Did the director keep you waiting more than a few minutes when you arrived?

- Did the director give you all the time you needed to talk about the program and answer all your questions?

- Did she show you the school's Mission Statement?

- Did she give you a booklet containing information about the school?

- Did she offer to supply you with references?

- At first glance, does the preschool look clean?

- Does it smell clean?

- Is the preschool licensed by the state?

- Is the license posted?

- If no, why not?

- Does the school do background checks before hiring teachers?

- What kind of experience do the teachers have?

The Infant Room

- Is the infant room clean?

- Are the electric outlets covered?

- Do the cabinets have childproof locks on them?

- Do you see any cleaning spray bottles sitting on the counters?

- Do you see anything that would be dangerous lying around in baby's reach?

- Are the counters clean and uncluttered?

- Are the diaper changing tables clean?

- Are there disposable gloves available for diaper changing?

- Is there a crib for each baby?

- Are the cribs in good condition? (Test them to make sure they're not wobbly or have any loose screws.)

- Are there enough high chairs or a feeding table for mealtimes?

- Are there enough swings, Exersaucers, bouncy seats, teething toys, stroller, etc. available for the babies?

- Is the above equipment in good condition?

- Are the toys and equipment age appropriate?

- Are the toys and equipment cleaned with bleach water each day?

- Is there a bin to put dirty toys that are used during the day? (For dropped toys, or toys that other babies put in their mouths.)

- Is there happy music playing in the room or lullabies if it is naptime?

- Is there a fire exit door with a sign posted above it?

- Does the room look like a place that your baby could have fun, explore and blossom?

- Do you have an overall good feeling about the room?

Staff

- Is there at least one child care provider for every four babies?

- Do the same caregivers take care of the same babies each day?

- Do different teachers come in for the late shift?

- Do all the teachers and caregivers have CPR and First Aid Certification?

- Are the caregivers friendly and eager to tell you about themselves and the program?

- Do the caregivers act in a professional manner?

- Do the caregivers look neat and clean and dressed appropriately?

- Are the caregivers warm and responsive to your baby when you visit?

- Do they know what to do if a baby is choking?

- Do they tell you about the daily activities?

- Do they take the babies outside, play music, do tummy time, etc.?

- Do they have specialists that come in for music, movement, etc.?

- Do they send home daily reports?

- Do they **want to know** your baby's schedule at home?

- Do they want to know how <u>**you**</u> soothe your baby when she is irritable or crying?

- What is their illness policy?

- Are there conferences or just daily check-ins?

- Are you allowed to talk directly with the teacher by phone or just the director if you need to call?

- What are their rules for visiting your baby at school?

- What is the policy for drop-off and pick-up?

- If someone else needs to pick up your baby, do they need a special card, password, driver's license, etc.?

- What type of security system do they use during school hours?

- Do they use the same substitutes all the time, so they get to know the babies and their schedules?

- Do you have an overall good feeling about the caregivers and the infant room?

Blythe's Final Thoughts:

- Did you get the cold shoulder or feel like they are too busy and you are unimportant?
  FIND ANOTHER PRESCHOOL

- What if, once your child is enrolled, you are told you *can't* visit anytime after all?
  FIND ANOTHER PRESCHOOL

- What if the facility looks, smells or feels dirty?
  FIND ANOTHER PRESCHOOL

- What if the caregivers are dressed inappropriately?
  FIND ANOTHER PRESCHOOL.

- What if the staff seems unhappy and not having fun?
  FIND ANOTHER PRESCHOOL

If you think you like the preschool after your first visit, drop in again (but this time unannounced). And if you have any remaining questions, call and get answers before you make a decision.

The most important question is would you feel good about leaving your precious baby at this preschool every day? If you feel **Great** about the preschool, then sign the papers. But if something feels amiss, even if you can't figure out what it is, always go with your gut instinct. It's almost always right.

Above all, you want to be able to enjoy watching your baby blossom in her new environment and feel good that you made the right decision.

Child Myth #1
Labor ends when the baby is born.

The following two chapters are experiences, feelings, and tips from new mommies and daddies. Some of them will have you shaking your head in agreement and all of them will warm your heart.
Enjoy!

What Mommies and Daddies Really Think

MOMMIES SHARE

When I asked new mommies questions about parenthood, here are some of their replies . . .

When I first saw my baby, I felt:
- Disbelief, couldn't stop smiling.
- Numb.
- Guilty for not having immediate bonding and mother instincts, amazed, excited.

When I first brought the baby home, I felt:
- Awesome, elated and emotional, overwhelmed, there were no more nurses to call for help.

When I was alone with the baby the first time I felt:
- Very comfortable with the baby but desperate about how I was going to take care of myself; eating, showering, etc.

- I was afraid to drive alone with baby and needed to bring grandmas with me for a long while.

- Peaceful, we listened to music.

Did you read anything helpful while you were pregnant:
- *Girlfriends' Guide to Pregnancy* by Vicki Iovine.

- I stopped reading everything as it became very scary and negative, too much conflicting information.

Did you nurse, and if so, how did you feel:
- Yes, for the first three months and really enjoyed the great feeling of bonding. It was also nice at night not having to get out of bed to warm a bottle.

- I nursed for four days to please my husband, but my heart wasn't in it. I felt better when I decided to give her a bottle and was very comfortable with making my own decision for my body.

When the baby is crying , I:
- Go through the checklist: wet, poopy, hungry, gas, tired, uncomfortable with her outfit, etc., and then sing songs to her. If everything checks out, I rock her.

- Stroke light circles on her back.

- Swaddle her and place her on top of the running dryer and use a pacifier if needed. Call the doctor for reassurance if she doesn't stop after an hour.

- Call or e-mail Blythe (the author).

I get my baby to sleep by:
- Letting her sleep in our bed.

- Feeding her a warm bottle, laying her down in the crib, playing soft music, and dimming the lights.

- Kissing her little fingers and nursing her.

I get my baby to eat by:
- She eats when she is hungry, no floor show needed.

- Pretending to drink the bottle first and making yummy sounds.

Are there any resources you wished you had looked into before the baby was born:
- Babycenter.com and preschool programs in my area.

- Information about the differences in raising a girl versus a boy.

The most difficult thing about having a baby is:
- Scheduling, balancing, and learning there is time for everything.

- Always wondering if you are doing it right.

- Losing the independence of coming and going when you want.

- Making appointments without worrying about day care hours.

- Less time for myself.

The most joyous thing about having a baby is:
- To see her face everyday and hear her sweet little voice.

- To watch her grow and learn new things.

- To watch her interact and respond to daddy.

- Watching her develop intelligence and knowing she is healthy and happy.

Day care is the place to:
- Learn to socialize, trust others.

- Have the care givers play and teach her new things.

- Learn mommy and daddy will always come back.

Most important piece of advice to pass on to a new parent:
- Enjoy everything you have been given and don't sweat the small stuff.

- Use your instincts. All babies are different and that is what makes them so great!

- Relax and know that as long as they are happy you are doing fine.

- Be patient when good-intentioned people give you their advice and know this is your child and you can do what you feel is right.

- Don't get stressed when all other people want to talk about is the baby and you want to talk about other real-life happenings also.

- Realize that this is the most glorious experience in your life.

Are there any shortcuts or tips for new parents:

- Sleeping with your newborn allows bonding.

- Have water pre-measured in the bottles for those middle of the night feedings.

- Always have the diaper bag packed and ready to go.

- Organize things the night before if you have to take the baby to day care (clothes, diaper bag, food, etc.)

MOTHER: Defined

A woman named Jean was renewing her driver's license at the county clerk's office. She was asked by the recorder to state her occupation. She hesitated, uncertain how to define herself.

"What I mean," explained the recorder, "do you have a job, or are you just a housewife?"

"Of course, I have a job," snapped Joan. "I'm a mother."

"We don't list 'mother' as an occupation, 'housewife' covers it," said the recorder, emphatically.

I forgot all about her story until one day I found myself in the same office. The employee there was obviously a career woman, poised and efficient, and who possessed a high sounding title that I think was something like Official Interrogator or Town Registrar.

" What is your occupation?" she said.

What made me say it, I do not know. The words simply popped out.

"I'm a Research Associate in the field of Child Development and Human Relations."

The clerk paused, ballpoint frozen in midstroke and looked up as though she had not heard right.

I repeated slowly, emphasizing the most significant words. Then I stared with wonder as my words were recorded in bold, black ink on the official questionnaire.

"Might I ask," said the clerk with new interest, "just how do you get into your field?"

Coolly, without any trace of fluster in my voice, I replied, "I began with a minor in sex and then a continuing program of research both in the laboratory and in the field, (normally I would have said indoors and out). I'm now working on my Masters (the whole darned family), and already have four ongoing projects (that is, four daughters). Of course, the job is one of the most demanding in the humanities. (Would any mother care to disagree?) And I often work 14-18 hours a day (24 is more like it). But the job is more challenging than most run-of-the-mill careers, and the rewards are more of a satisfaction, rather than just the money.

There was an increasing note of respect in the clerk's voice as she completed the form, stood up, and personally ushered me to the door.

As I drove into our driveway, buoyed up by my glamorous

new career, I was greeted by my lab assistants, ages thirteen, seven, and three. Upstairs I could hear our new experiment, (a six-month-old) in the child-development program, testing out a new vocal pattern.

I felt triumphant. I had scored a beat on bureaucracy. I had gone on the official records as someone more distinguished and indispensable to mankind than "just another mother."

Motherhood, what a glorious career! Especially when there's a title on the door. Does this make grandmothers "Senior Research Associates" in the field of Child Development and Human Relations? Yes and great grandmothers are "Executive Senior Research Consulting Associates." No question about it.

I also think it makes aunts "Associate Research Advisors."

As told by Kathy

DADDIES SHARE

When I asked new daddies questions about parenthood, here are some of their replies . . .

When I first found out I was going to be a daddy, I felt:
- Happy, scared, shocked, disbelief
- Excited, knowing that my life was about to change.

I prepared by doing the following:
- Bought and read books.
- Went to the gym.
- Took baby classes.
- Talked about it to anyone that would listen.
- Researched everything, personal lives, finance, marriage, things to ensure a healthy baby.
- Looked at lots of online resources.

My biggest concern was:
- Potential birth defects.
- Real-life responsibility.
- My age. Was I too old to have a baby?
- Something could happen to my wife and/or baby.

When I first saw my baby, I felt:
- Happy, anxious, joy, pride.
- In shock, I didn't know a newborn could have a cone head.

The most difficult thing about having a baby is:
- Nothing. Just be patient in everything you do.
- Time, the old life is gone forever.
- Not knowing why the baby was crying.

The best thing about having a baby is:
- The joy of having a new life.
- Being responsible for raising your wonderful gift is the best.
- The smiles and coos of joy when I sing to him.
- Watching him develop and accomplish new tasks.
- The love, satisfaction, and being able to care for such a precious thing.
- Seeing her beautiful smile takes away any bad day I may have.

My special tips are:
- Always involve your baby in everything. If you eat, have your baby sitting in the infant seat, if she is awake. Expose her to everything, take advantage of every opportunity that will allow her to utilize her senses.
- Learn the football hold.

- Get organized with a routine.
- Sing, sing, sing to her. Act silly and just have fun!

When my baby is crying I:
- Pick her up and distract her.
- I don't run to her in a panic. I just walk calmly and talk softly.
- Check her diaper and when she was last fed.
- Wrap her in a blanket, turn on the dryer, and lay her on top of it. The vibration calms her (and don't leave her).
- Find mommy.

Day care is a place for the baby to:
- Be in a stimulating, safe environment other than our home.
- To have social interaction.
- Gain independence from mommy and daddy.
- Have some great learning experiences.

If I had one tip to pass on it would be:
- When you are feeding baby, try and keep her awake the entire feeding. I take off her socks and tickle her feet to keep her awake.
- I found the book *On Becoming Baby Wise* by Gary Ezzo really helped. Eat, play, sleep. That was the best routine for our newborn. He did much better when we played with him after he ate, even if we had to take off his socks or move him

around a bit to keep him awake. The big payoff was that he ate more at one sitting, was happier during playtime, and consistently fell asleep one-half hour to forty-five minutes after playing. This worked every time for our baby.

- Throw out everything you thought would work and be flexible.
- Relax and have fun. You probably know more than you think you do.
- No two babies are the same, just go with your heart and your instincts.

FOOTPRINTS

Walk a little slower,
Daddy, said a child so
small. I'm following in your footsteps and
I don't want to fall.

Sometimes your steps are very fast,
Sometimes they're hard to see;
So walk a little slower, Daddy,
For you are leading me.

Someday when I'm all grown up,
You're what I want to be;
Then I will have a child
Who'll want to follow me.

I want to lead just right,
And know that I was true;
So, walk a little slower, Daddy,
For I must follow you.

Author unknown

"I always wondered what her secrets were, now I know. The household was always so organized as Blythe dealt with the babies in stride. The children turned out great and I kept my sanity during those baby years!"

Sam Lipman (former husband)
Scottsdale, AZ

"Husbands, let your wife have a day off. When you are home alone with your new baby, this great book will help you get through the day. It's a must have for all new fathers."

M. Todd Arak, D.M.D.
Scottsdale, AZ

I don't know how I would have gotten through those cranky nights without the tips in this book. My baby loved being swaddled in a warm, toasty blanket. This should be every new Mom's Baby Manual!

Arlene K
Moorestown, New Jersey

My Mom is the greatest when it comes to baby care. I've grown up watching her in action. It's amazing how she always knows just what to do to make her babies happy. I was the luckiest baby in the world!

Andrew Lipman, son
New York, New York

A Few More Tips to Make Life Easier

A FEW MORE TIPS TO MAKE YOUR LIFE EASIER
Blythe's Favorites

- When changing the baby and she is really squirmy, take her arms and wrap them in the bottom of her shirt or a "onesie" (see *Glossary*) like a jelly roll. This will keep those hands out of the dirty diaper. Sing songs, do nursery rhymes, tickle her, do anything to make diapering a positive experience.

- When the baby sleeps, take a 20-minute power nap. You come first, not the housework, bills, or cooking. Your chores will still be there when you wake up and when you're rested, they will seem more manageable.

- Plan at least two hours a week just for you. Hire a baby-sitter one afternoon a week. Stay home and read, take a bath, sit outside, call girlfriends, get a manicure. Just pamper yourself. No working, as this is your special time. I used to get girls from the YMCA baby-sitting course. It was very affordable, great experience for them, and gave me time while still being close by if a question should arise.

- Keep the camera out, ready, loaded with film, and batteries charged. You never know when there will be a moment you will want to capture forever.

- When you come home from an outing, repack the bag immediately, so you will be ready for the next time.

- Keep a change of *your* clothes in the trunk of your car. You'll be glad you have them when baby decides to decorate you with her lunch.

- Don't forget to eat. You need your energy to take care of your baby and stay healthy.

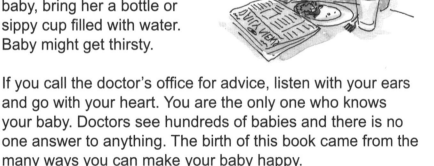

- When you go out with the baby, bring her a bottle or sippy cup filled with water. Baby might get thirsty.

- If you call the doctor's office for advice, listen with your ears and go with your heart. You are the only one who knows your baby. Doctors see hundreds of babies and there is no one answer to anything. The birth of this book came from the many ways you can make your baby happy.

Here is the most important piece of advice I can give you:

Don't forget to take care of yourself. Be proud of who you are as a wife, mother, and as a woman; or as a husband, father, and as a man. Make your heart smile by enjoying each and every minute you spend with your baby. Life is wonderful!

Your most precious commodity, your baby. There is nothing more exciting on earth than to have the opportunity to watch her grow, explore, and learn. To have the opportunity to expose her to all the good things life has to offer. To have the opportunity to teach her all you know. And most of all, to relax, have fun, and enjoy this miracle you have created.

I hope this book has provided you with some useful tips to help make your parenthood experience a little easier. If you discover other tips that would be helpful to new parents, please e-mail them to me at Blythe@babyinstructions.com. I will post them along with tips from other parents on my website, www.babyinstructions.com. Thank you for sharing. Please visit my website for additional instructions on raising a happy, healthy baby.

Glossary

GLOSSARY

binky (*also pacifier*)—a nipple mounted on a circular plastic ring. The baby can suck on this without getting air into her tummy. Used to pacify babies.

Boppy Pillow®—a horseshoe-shaped pillow used to place the baby on when nursing. You may also lay the baby on her back on this pillow and put a toy overhead. It works well when baby is starting to hold her bottle and does not want mommy or daddy to hold her.

bouncy seat—a seat into which an infant is placed. Soft fabric creates a comfortable environment for newborns to feed, sleep, and play.

Exersaucer®—a portable seat that allows the baby to spin around, play with toys, bounce, and rock. It has a three-position height adjustment, and three flip-down feet for stationary position, as well as interactive toys on the tray.

fitness ball—a large rubber ball used in gyms to exercise.

jelly roll—to take a blanket, towel, or piece of fabric and, starting at one end, roll it up.

mobile—a decorative structure suspended from the baby's crib. It may have a music box attached and a spring that makes it go around.

onesie—a one-piece outfit that goes over the head and snaps under the legs.

receiving blanket—a soft, cotton or flannel blanket about 1/4-inch thick.

Snugli®—a baby carrier made of fabric. It has two straps that go over your shoulders and wrap around your waist and holding an attached seat. The baby can sit facing either front or back, depending on which type of Snugli you purchase.

swaddle—to wrap the baby tightly in a blanket to restrict movement.

wedge—a piece of fabric-covered foam with four points and a flat bottom. This product comes with two wedges attached by Velcro, leaving a space to put the baby in between (on her back or side) to prevent rolling onto her tummy.

ABOUT THE AUTHOR

An Infant Care Specialist, Blythe Lipman has worked with babies for over twenty years. Meeting her first baby when she was eleven years old, she soon became her neighborhood's favorite baby-sitter. She continued her love for babies while she was in college and beyond, always knowing just what they needed. Blythe volunteered in the Neonatal Intensive Care Unit in Boston's Lying-In Hospital while attending Boston University in 1972. She was also awarded a Supplemental Child Development Associate Certificate in 1999. She has continued caring for babies as the CEO of many infant rooms in preschools throughout the country. She is also a management consultant, helping to set up smoothly functioning and professionally-run infant rooms in preschools. Blythe has worked extensively with new parents providing workshops, in-home visits, tips, and daily phone calls of assurance. Blythe has two grown children and lives in Scottsdale, Arizona, with her partner Gary and puppy Lucy.

To contact Blythe and receive free monthly tips send your email address to **babyinstructions@cox.net** and take a peek at her website: **www.babyinstructions.com**. She would love to hear from you!

Order Form

To order additional copies of *More Help! My Baby Came Without Instructions:*

By phone : 480-510-1453

Online : Visit www.babyinstructions.com to use Paypal
or contact babyinstructions@cox.net

By mail: Complete the order form below and mail to:

      Baby Instructions
      17743 N. 81st Way
      Scottsdale, AZ 85255

Name: _____

Address: _____

City_____ State: _____ Zip: _____

Telephone : _____

E-mail: _____

Payment Information:
Please make checks or money orders payable to: Baby Instructions

_____Copies @ $14.95 $_____
     Shipping   4.00 $_____
       Total $_____

Thank your for your order.
Blythe